D0929604

VENICE

ANGE MLINKO

Farrar
Straus
Giroux

NEW
YORK

Farrar, Straus and Giroux
120 Broadway, New York 10271

Library of Congress Cataloging-in-Publication Data
Names: Mlinko, Ange, author.
Title: Venice : poems / Ange Mlinko.
Description: First edition. | New York : Farrar, Straus and Giroux, 2022.
Identifiers: LCCN 2021052094 | ISBN 9780374604004 (hardcover)
Subjects: LCGFT: Poetry.
Classification: LCC PS3563.L58 V46 2022 | DDC 811/.54—dc23
LC record available at https://lccn.loc.gov/2021052094

Designed by Crisis

Our books may be purchased in bulk for promotional, educational, or
business use. Please contact your local bookseller or the Macmillan
Corporate and Premium Sales Department at 1-800-221-7945, extension
5442, or by email at MacmillanSpecialMarkets@macmillan.com.

www.fsgbooks.com
www.twitter.com/fsgbooks
www.facebook.com/fsgbooks

1 3 5 7 9 10 8 6 4 2

TO MY SONS

For that was the charm—that so preposterously, with the
essential notes of the impression so happily struck, the velvet
air, the extravagant plants, the palms, the oranges, the cacti,
the architectural fountain, the florid local monument,
the cheap and easy exoticism, the sense as of people feeding,
off in the background, very much al fresco, *that is on*
queer things and with flaring lights—one might
almost have been in a corner of Naples or of Genoa.

—Henry James, *The American Scene*

CONTENTS

....

It is almost the new year. Almost . . . **3**

VENICE

It is almost the new year. Almost
a new decade—and good riddance
to the old one. We go, on a whim,
to a Mycenaean pit that made compost
out of a king, his funerary conveyance,
and the living horses that drew him.

But Famagusta . . . can you say
by what ghost we are detained
at the place where the Venetians
witnessed the Ottomans flay
their commander? It has rained:
clover makes handsome reparations,

and butterflies called painted ladies
are visiting their yellow cups on stalks,
one by one. Fennel sends up plumes.
My kids fill their lungs, stretch their bodies,
roll in long grass amid half-hidden rocks,
while I wander the dank castle rooms,

surfacing on a rampart where the sea
is militantly blue, the sun a medallion.

A whitecap's surrendering tower,
a glitter as of weaponry,
rehearse their capacity to stun:
every wave has a will to power.

(Cyprus, Boxing Day, 2009)

PART I

VENUS

SCALES AND PROBABILITY

....

I

In or around 1929 the character of dreams changed.
The collision of Fermi and Respighi on the *Conte Verde*.
As the ocean liner churned its ghostly foam,
the man who had X-rayed crystals admitted an immunity
to music. The man who had scored the *Fountains of Rome*
could not explain musical properties in terms of physics.
They shuffled irreconcilable domains like steamer chairs
until Argentina loomed. Two men in the arms of a galaxy.

Fermi returned to his pions and muons, Respighi to a com-
position in D major. The dependable staff
of sheet music paper, like a ship's railing, steadied him.
Fermi went on to lend his name to a formal paradox:
given the scale of the universe, the probability of life
elsewhere couldn't be squared with its failure to find us.

II

Fermi irradiated paraffin, aluminum, marble,
wood. Recorded the speed of particle decay for each.

Respighi, joking to Puccini, introduced his "half a wife,"
newlyweds between double ceremonies
at the registry office and "Rome's smallest church."
A year before he died, Elsa wrote in her journal:
"Today I am 41. . . . Words can never describe this
. . . boundless bliss" at sharing the maestro's life.

He "always travelled with a small compass,"
so that he could sleep, whenever possible,
with his body on a north-south axis;
their wellness tips were a mutual espousal.
Her quinsy, his flu; her colitis, his migraine.
Vesuvio smoked like uncorked champagne.

III

After paging through *La Primavera* with less comprehension
than awe at the three-stranded braid of music and German/
Italian librettos—for which the words *Träume* and *sogno*
stood in microcosm—I sat outside the library at a sinkhole
encircled by palms, ferns, and moss. A little blue heron
(not, as I first thought, a baby "great" blue heron)
was trying to keep a low profile in the shallows,
perfectly still except for the ripples of invisible darters

that seemed to be kissing the surface from the other side.
I too was all blue, down to the stone in my Roman ring.
And then a cardinal joined us, male and proud,
adding his burly nuptial chirp to a scene I was sorry
to leave, but a violet rain cloud was lowering.
I just made it to my car when the pelting started.

THE PSYCHIC CAPITAL
OF THE WORLD

Summer. A toad died in a plastic habitat,
sparrow nestlings in the grille fledged,
the Don Juan rose's ups and downs
were managed with a spritz of sulfur at
intervals, the St. Augustine was edged;
and at the crossroads of the town

there was almost nothing to trumpet
the psychic capital of the world, albeit
a unified aesthetic seemed to have bled
from a great purple pen, whose *stet*
could be read in the sign-up sheet
and handcrafted amethyst death's-head.

The dead had gone abroad while
vegetation marched on the veranda.
We imagined that they had surpassed,
by six time zones or so, a period style
on a transatlantic seesaw,
so much was our present their past—

settee, drapery, glassed-in bookshelf.
I expected a medium in a shawl
to materialize from behind
a piano—which no doubt played itself—
waving her eye of crystal
(atoms, if not planets, aligned) . . .

Lovers are perched on the rim of a storm.
In the gale, the Don Juan rose
thrashes a dozen siren blooms.
At the same time the roselike form
of love's disturbance bursts windows
along the shore it hugs and dooms.

There is a legal matter to attend to;
an old pact you must put asunder.
It contributes to the rut you're in.
Is that a seagull or a sprig of mistletoe
you've managed to palely loiter under?
By summer you'll cross an ocean.

The regional airport gets little traffic—
if you hear a plane, it's probably yours.
Distance would seem to abolish
the distinction between aircraft
and the bright scumble of the stars,
but a ticket goes much farther than a wish.

In your aura, no doctors or creditors.
Somewhere the sphinx moth is darting,
the clothes fall at your feet loud as snow
—who knows down what acoustic corridors?
Nor will the sadness of your parting
rise above the decibels of velcro.

THE GATES OF HELL

(Rodin)

He didn't mean these kinds of gates.
But here we are. Or I mean I.
On these darkest days of the year,
the sun shows that it accommodates
our needs, and turns itself on high.
Show me, sun, what I am doing here.

I've been thinking for some time
about *Fallen Caryatid*, shouldering
her capital. Actually there were two—
the other bore an urn; they made a rhyme.
So did *Fugit Amor*, the enduring
nature of attraction to undo.

The traveling show, arrayed in
a gallery in Savannah, was a gift.
Now at the gates of an airport,
another Christmas traveler laden
with everything that should uplift,
I'm trying to be a good sport

on my first holiday without my kids.
The garbage trucks resume their rounds
on roads cellophaned with ice,
masticating packaging like chrysalids
summarily shaken for sounds
or weighed in the hand for the size

of the happiness underneath . . .
I steer my thoughts back to the show
of misery beyond measurement
between gates which bequeath
images of angel wings working to slow
a fall, not maneuver an ascent.

The sun that cuff-links a hill's white sleeve,
the plane that bootstraps us to the sky,
neither is adequate to the human need
individual to each of us here who leave
someone else behind to cry;
queued, with scarcely a line to read.

He removed *The Kiss* from the ensemble,
surmising correctly that naked bliss
was out of place at the gates of hell.
If it *is* bliss that makes us tremble;
if it is not, also, its own abyss
between two gates at a terminal.

The hotel showers were splendidly profligate.
The aqueduct that fed the big
fountains down the street probably ran underneath
my bed, giving the water pressure
a nice bump. These were veritable circuses of water:
crowds pleased to see, qua
the wonders of Roman hydraulic engineering,
water shatter its own mirror
never incurring bad luck. That weird accord
of rationality with credulity back
of everything; a double consciousness, sticky,
with surfacing its principal aesthetic.
It was the fountains that helped me remember
a spinto's stratagem
of holding her breath for at least four minutes,
training herself to dive in,
then, if not divadom. Naiads must be, conversely,
vocal masters.

What do they sing? They sing odes to the Pantheon,
whose niches stand empty
of the gods that a ray of sun through the oculus
goes on splashing with awful

clarity on its rounds of the heavens; the architect,
Hadrian, was the *passionate*
emperor. Another temple of his, nicked of its storied
goddesses ROMA and AMOR,
put to work the magical properties of palindromes
for the good of the state. A pet falcon
sacrificed so that its earthly years might be annexed
to the emperor's was a Five Year Plan;
never forget the desk blotter in the administrative
office was blood red. I conflate
it with the rosebushes at the House of the Vestals.
Twice I saw a bride dressed
up, toddling in the street, posing for photographs,
and if they turn up in *Vogue*,
I won't be the wiser. On close inspection,
those holes that fleck
the ancient masonry weren't made by bullets,
but hooks that secured the marble.

Monumental doors testify to the height of the heroes
that walk the earth then disappear.
Now what are the odds that the moon in a pellucid
cerulean dusk shakes loose
as a disc of marble spolia? It's all a psychic recyclable
that seems endlessly up for grabs.
The Romans exit doors sideways, like cats flattening
themselves on a ledge, then

venture boldly into traffic. If a sudden access of quiet
obtains, it's in a square of colossi
where executions took place. The windswept expanse
is both style and semantics.

So, up glaring stairs, in a killing sun, I hazarded
my life for a snatched reward
at the door handle with brass asps intertwined,
under ceilings some painter
wanted to strike us all blind with. ("Con forza!")
On the outdoor screens a new horror
was unscrolling from America, and conversations
with no calls to punish or pray
broke out all around me, in English, putting emphasis
on pragmatics. What has
reason to do with our touristing in the ruins
over which a seagull made a *W*
—or was it a bent drill bit, a (sorry) *augur*?
Or that the back catalog
of songs in the temples' open cellae was amplified
to drown out loss of life,
with empty trays carried aloft by pine trees high
in the hills, listing like Corybantes?

DUCKS

....

After the olivine waves of Marina di Torre del Lago,
we drive between colonnades of umbrella pines . . .
It is 7:30 p.m. and the midsummer sun has just descended
below the tree line . . . Lorenzo laments that the days
are getting shorter now. I think this is premature.
By our separate doors we leave the Fiat together.

The roadside broom and bluets seem to go together,
but past the threshold of the estate nothing is allowed to go
to picturesque ruin, and nothing runs riot. Mature
magnolias line the long approach to the villa, spines
of stiff-leaved ground cover bristle; it's hardly paradise,
but I follow the gravel path to the single palm descended

from its paradisiacal prototype . . . The yard is scented
with thyme, and classical music as if from the ether
sounds from a distance; speakers might have risen to a dais,
but now there are speakers in the trees! Not long ago,
I would have been enchanted; yet even as one who pines
for the absolute, I don't want to make a premature

assessment of the villa's charms before I make a tour
of its offerings. It faces us as a goddess who condescended,

once upon a time, to face the photographers. Lorenzo opines
that Puccini was always hunting something, with either
rifles or leitmotif . . . Eventually we pass—*Prego!*—
through a portal, our uneasy little pas de deux

crumbling as we transition in a kind of sultry daze
from the vacant frontage with its orchestral imprimatur
to a backyard soundstage, a top-forty number and a go-go
troupe of girls dancing in sync. Mothers have descended
on the place with aunties, nanas, sparsely seated together
in rows of ordinary folding chairs that are hard on lower spines.

Lorenzo is galvanized by the sight. He pines
for something less abstract—where are the does
of yesteryear? . . . I wander off, aware of being thrust together
under artificial conditions, bored with this amateur
production . . . It's an ennui so blank and open-ended,
it derives more from Antonioni than ego.

Ergo the pines, descended into premature darkness
under a spot of smelted apricot in the west. We bid adieus
together to swan-head spigots. And a wall of fig leaves . . .

Here where the various Venuses gather
—you know the types: one kind
posing with a dolphin or a scallop shell,
another gyring to look at her behind,
another, a more modest bather,
crossing her arms—a church bell

coincides with the approach of sirens,
pitting emergency against eternity;
and the sand is cinders and glitter,
the source of which everyone can see
towering over the environs:
the volcano, arch-depositor

of new earth over old. As if a sapphire
beckoned with an aquamarine finger,
one wave and the Venus undoing her sandal
leaps up, on the beach of hot clinker,
walking barefoot to a blue that will suspire
into the sky with a hiss of scandal.

As if the sand weren't hot enough,
the city streets are paved with lava flags,
and as if a volcano did not suffice,
fireworks branch like cave-paint stags
jumping in brief bursts above the roof,
almost nightly, fizzling out in paradise.

This is why, given the charcoal black,
the heat which comes from below
as much as from the sun in July,
it's strange that Venus should go
where even the butterflies are flak
to ask her husband for jewelry.

He who made a shield for Achilles
might armor his wife with a bangle.
But tasting Solfatara in her throat,
she cannot disentangle
invasive, owl-infested trees
making an opportunistic moat

around the stinking fumaroles,
and the cessation of cicadas.
Venus wonders why she's come.
The perfume of their fermatas
is that of the mute illegible scrolls
charred in Herculaneum.

She couldn't say what she envisioned:
something machine-precisioned,
exciting envy; her personal signature,
a sacrificial ziggurat in miniature,
the thong sandaling a horse bodily,
his pièce de résistance of theophany.

When her husband presents her,
at last, with his gift—a necklace
of lava beads—does she laugh,
or shudder? Oubliette to a necropolis,
memento mori, vanity's censure,
it says he's in the mud for love.

And seeing her expression, he coos:
if you don't like this one, I've got another—
(which I saw like a birth, dear reader)
a blood-red moon, forged from either
—roughly—the flank of Vesuvius,
or the heart of the creator.

LA CASA DEL DIAVOLO

··

I

Dear A.—Nailing crockery to the walls
was not something I ever understood.
But Simonetta's majolica falls,
like this sideboard, painted wood,
under the enchantment of a freehand look—
a curling script, a loose grape tendril,
the form that hecatomb smoke took
purling to a Roman god's nostril . . .

Because geranium is crinkled
in the spillage from the wishing well,
now outdated and backfilled,
this whole place evinces the nature
of a souvenir plate. Another tell:
the mosquito flourish in its signature.

II

The rustic bicycle, like a pen
that spent its ink, wrote an invisible sentence

to the ramparts and back, now and again
rolling through the arches of an aqueduct
dowsing with its sixth sense
across the hillsides. Locals tucked
plastic water bottles under spouts
chiseled into lions' pouts

stationed at intervals, like shrines.
Their cars idled while they stooped,
and on Sundays formed lines.
They trust this water more, Lorenzo whooped,
than what comes out of their taps?
The sources snake beneath the maps.

III

The little terrier Amore, they warned me,
had eaten the seat belts; so there I was,
friend, fearing whiplash in the backseat
(no headrest either!), in all respects afloat—
Simonetta on alert for signs of gallantry,
like the wives of those diminished Casanovas
who dream they've merely grown discreet.
And the dissertation she once wrote

on courtesan-poetesses, fancying herself
of that ilk ("Like me!"—a phrase she'd strew
among her compliments), gathers dust on a shelf.
When I think of Boccherini's metacarpals
interred beneath the soppressata marbles
of the duomo, I think: *Casa del Diavolo.* Those two.

We were, you might say, dangling over the buried city.
If this villa had a cellar, its floor would be the ceiling
—tap it—to another, in shallow strata, but irreality
in this case went all the way down, then back up, reeling
(so to speak) in the accoutrements of a lost beau monde.
Who was I there? A guest, a voyeur, a vagabond.

The sitting part of the sitting room dominated
by two grand pianos was—marginal. Like black mirrors,
their lids pooled the light. Was it here the walls were red?
The other parlor was powder blue, a style in arrears
to a dynasty gone to dust. Each room staged a dialogue
between colors with a touch of fop, a wink of rogue:

a lilac wall beside a raisin daybed; saffron upholstery
with sapphire mural, or celadon via mauve.
A Baccarat chandelier bestowed a frozen curtsy.
The dinner service Romanov,
the chairs a gift from the last queen of Italy . . .
As I say it had the air of irreality.

But any air of decadence it might have possessed
was doused by a melancholic sense of paradox
partly from what lay underground, and for the rest
by the propinquity of large apartment blocks,
their laundry beaten by the bay breeze
sieved through satellite dishes and balconies.

No, he would not play for us.—As if to resist
discomfiture, either in the bold request or its denial,
he told that his grandmother, trained as a harpist,
gave up the instrument when a growing profile
of (unnamed) misfortunes accrued to her performance.
And even this superstition was part of the romance:

Though he'd never heard her play, he arrived
at his own vocation through primogeniture,
and it was indeed in this house that she'd lived;
he slept in the last room where they found her.
She was the genius of accumulated shrines.
Instead of household gods there were nine felines.

I suppose I missed the moral of the unheard harp.
But the rescues I had earlier witnessed
—the frescoes—caught me in a perspectival warp
which as each tinted scene evanesced
belied the claim that they emerged from time:
they were dying back into the old regime.

And when I aired my dismay at the waste,
the language barrier was thinnest just then, and *No,*
his bafflement said, *your perturbation is misplaced.*
"Not wasted, but preserved by the volcano.
All that sublime you saw would have been lost."
—Echoing with an unheard *almost, almost, almost.*

These bareback races are medieval
in the modern sense: a bribe, a ruse,
the occasional fall, fracture, and a bullet

—but also in the sense of a retrieval
of standards and emblems, the use
of symbol, allegory, amulet,

the team colors you cannot refuse.
Tomorrow the terra-cotta dust
will plume for about two minutes

taking the imprint of horseshoes.
The beasts will reslot themselves addorsed
in bays like a train line terminus . . .

Stone palazzi keep their iron rings,
which served as hitching posts,
antiquated and ornamental,

rusted and simple, the kinds of things
the eye probes for the ghosts
of the enduring and the gentle.

Ahead of me walks an elderly pair,
divorced in the modern sense:
she employs him to manage her condo,

keep the villa in good repair,
till from tax exile (an expense
of spirit in the wastes of Monte Carlo)

she returns, scattering guests
with her dogs and her armory
of caustic appraisals and lightly flung

(as he scoops up her favorite) jests:
"Ah, you're just his type, Amore—
long brown hair, and much too young."

SLEEPWALKING IN VENICE

Two kinds of imagination: the strong, the promiscuous.
—Giacomo Leopardi

CALLE ROMBIASIO

Watching a boneless nymph's
halfhearted resurrection
from a spout in the pavement
over and over; catching a glimpse
of the source of my exhaustion,
as if my gaze all this time had lent

muscular support to her effort . . .
She wasn't at all as mischievous
as her sisters, who seeped up
through the flagstones of the court,
serving the blue basilica to us
repurposed as a teacup.

Nor was she splenetic as
the poltergeist in the moka pot,
seething liquid from every fissure,

then exploding on its ring of gas.
If it seemed that water was fraught
with divinities under pressure,

maybe I was going mad myself,
just a little, in this hall of mirrors.
So much glass my eyes glazed over,
and green waves laminating a shelf
where recto sits, and verso appears
in blinding dazzle seeking cover.

Such a surplus of marble that
even in the apartment I occupied
(no palazzo), the stairs luminesced;
if, as Michelangelo had thought,
an angel lurked within, it was mortified
under the tread of a houseguest.

But when I reached the door,
sprung the lock, climbed the last
spiral flight through thin air,
it was to a wheelhouse (more
or less) of a vessel held fast
to its view of the *sestiere*;

and I was alone with the seagulls,
listening to the creaking ropes

of dinghies below, whose sway
I felt—impossibly—in lulls
unaddressed as sails, or hopes:
tethered to my getaway.

SAN MARCO

Morning glory folded in the scrolls
of columns dissolved their claims
to mass in a bisque-blue apparition;
dusk would blur the ink on rolls
recording their angelic names:
Fra Lippo Lapis, *Azure-Titian* . . .
like the boaters with their poles,
and not unlike the playground games

where you sidestep the cracks,
or leapfrog stepping-stones,
I tested substantiality bit by bit
with my whole body. Bones
of the duomo melt; how stacks
my hazy realness against it?

SCALA D'ORO

I climbed the Golden Staircase.
Hadn't meant to. Who sightsees
in council chambers? . . . Blasé
toward doge, lawyer, and delegate,
the scoop of whispering galleries,
I was arrested by the gilded vault
where images of Venus and her cult
were preamble to affairs of state.

Head tipped back, hand gripping rail . . .
I was bowled over by the hubris.
Reached the antechamber reeling
at what hung in the balance: pale
throats bared, a puff piece
for the ages floating on the ceiling.

ANTECHAMBER, MAIN HALL

It struck me that there'd been a fire
in these rooms, if not a brawl.
More *scuro* than *chiaro* in the employ
of the magistrates, choirs
of angels boiled up to forestall

their double-dealings with trompe l'oeil.
Sooty gold-and-black marble conspires
to churn an atmosphere of upheaval . . .

Yes, this place was unwholesome.
I made out Hera gifting a peacock
to the republic. Her crowded bower
jostled, unanchored the gaze from
any mooring, put the whole baroque
in service to the reigning power.

COMPASS ROOM

"Imagine me as a three-dimensional chessboard
on which several dozen games are being played
around the clock, with multiple figures
whose functions take some up and down the board,
unconstrained by distances; others are confined to diagonals;
and some are either on foot or afloat but never both,
who rest in velvet-lined beds after harlequin day,
a moonlit sapphire set in windows nightly . . .

"A room sighs when a door is opened, closed.
I have hoarded all the thieves, swindlers, and traitors
in my iron stanzas like a bank vault, on the understanding

that a productive interest grows in the smallest cell;
that iniquity builds under pressure, from a principal;
that to someone powerful somewhere this is valuable."

PIAZZETTA

Canal steps troubled by centuries
and off-the-shoulder things
that scandalize the sanctuaries
lead, among the stony echoings,
to wisdom like *Never send an email*
when you're angry—and never
make a promise when you're happy. (Male
faces grinned.) *We should endeavor,*

one girl submitted, *to take a grain of salt*
with the outburst, the promise made in bed . . .
We should be trained to doubt; the default
will always be ardor. The cafés fed
their chatter into a cochlear gestalt,
a labyrinthine ear without thread.

VAPORETTO

No bellboys, no bellboys, I thought,
bumping the suitcase on each step,

not like Aschenbach (what had I brought?
my hand squeezed bloodless by the strap).
And having failed to tip and fall,
I gave a last heave, and pushed the thing . . .
it snapped open like an arsenal
of folded silks (for parachute landing

in the dark, with flare) . . . Meanwhile
the bell buoys in the lagoon recorded data
regarding tides, temperature, salinity,
the migratory sands . . . and if a regatta
glanced off a satellite into infinity,
it hung like a chandelier in time's exile.

ENVOI

She turned her ankle playing tennis
ten days before she was to go
on her first, lamentably shelved,
trip to Venice. How then is
she so long and so slow
to make amends with herself? . . .

Stepping back through the looking glass,
I'd tell my friends about the time
I made reservations for Venice,
then had to call them off seeing as

I couldn't negotiate the sublime
on crutches, after a bout of tennis

on an uneven Moroccan clay court
put my right ankle in a cast.
The rhyme surely made an imprecation,
a sort of curse-cum-tort,
as well as the fact that in contrast
to other sport, Venice is a game for one.

The stamp of the real authenticates
imagination's passport, I thought.
Yet as the train drew me backward
across the lagoon (whose cognates
include *lacuna*, of course), I fought
the cold, green voice that declared

It was as though she'd never been.
Yes? *Or it's that she went alone . . .*
and saw myself reflected nowhere,
deprived of some . . . vitamin . . .
like a vampire feeling her bones
that can't find herself in a mirror . . .

But did she (a funny thing to ask)
sleep deeply, as I see she dreamed well?
I know mon ange—*her elaborate schemes;*

and in the city of the erotic masque,
her blindfolds and foam plugs are farcical;
bat-spread blackout curtains figure in regimes

where a plan of action or program
to lose consciousness is no paradox.
Refrigeration, wrapped in a duvet, is ideal . . .
The light doze ends at 1 AM—
an existential cry from the clocks,
the gulling of a campanile.

CHIMENEA

I

A girl puked on the tour bus
on the switchback up Vesuvius.
Her mother looked the other way
—out the window. Where else?
Wildflowers, hardy and tender,
seemed unaware of the perils
of flourishing in cinder.

We trudged, as through beach sand,
and when we got back on, sand
had been shoveled onto the mess.
I got my contraband: pumice
out of the core's juices—color puce—
alarmingly warm from the crater,
that supreme indifferent *mater.*

II

Chimeneas were all the rage.
Hemispheric, the copper bowl

hung fire, like the globe:
a cross-sectioned model.

In the dark behind us, what?
Panthers, birds of prey.
Night inverts the hierarchy.
The flames of February purify

the pique, the umbrage, the stuffy
dreams, the nasal cathedral
close with incense. Hence
our embers spray and cleanse,

our ash an alkaline scrub.
Never mind the Pompeian brain
that turned to black glass—
a dark crystal ball wherein came to pass

the future: us, reflected in its sheen.
Having excavated his dream
(for we found the skeleton in bed),
we speculate now on papyrus scrolls

compressed into coded coals
that rose into the skies as smoke,
the burnt sacrifice of lyric,
ode, supplication, obloquy.

The log wouldn't take right away,
and we had no accelerant.
My son fetched dryer lint,
which did its voodoo. It burned
for the duration of a movie.
(Firecrackers, leftover, passé,
reminded us the year had turned

but wetly they popped, distant,
anticlimactic.) The full moon
was lost in cloud cover, mist,
winter's high dew point.
For as long as the hero kissed
the heroine, or a great fortune
was tied up in red tape,

we would hold out for the plot
which, abstracted to this,
was passion's caveat—
its propensity to ashes
swelling on a pillow of gases
then subsiding under the stars
and scouring meteors.

PART II

FLORIDA

Florida, venereal soil . . .

—Wallace Stevens

MOTH ORCHID

I like—don't you?—that it has an insect tattooed
in its sanctum sanctorum, a suitor's pseud.
That's one aspect of its ghostliness, its moon-tones,

its utter prescience, not to mention cojones.

For if those speckles don't answer to the footprints
of insects tramping through the moondust
of its pollen, I don't know what its six headdresses

are for, or what their iodine-and-moonlight tint redresses.

Nor why each of those hexa-heads tricks
in a slightly different direction, and mimics
a *Demoiselles d'Avignon* tableau

modulating to monstrousness from beauty.

Or say they mimic a mother's uncanny abilities,
such as vision in 360 degrees
(since this was a Mother's Day gift

which required equal parts extravagance and thrift).

Or say that the gift of a *moth* orchid
to the mother from her kid
encrypts something of her lonely midnight vigils,

the moon in varying dosages like Advils . . .

Because its soft tints and moon-tones
combine with its etymological cojones
to represent the parent who must hybridize

both mother and father in her kids' eyes.

....

Once more my unholy rose wrote
its signature on the back of my hand,
taking me for both paper and pen:
red ink. And once more
I watched the promissory note
unfold and read and did not understand:
"Change was always at your door,
dear heart: a blossom knocking itself open.

A mythical creature, like the basilisk
or helldog (I bloom in triplicate) . . .
for all that you brought me morning coffee
(espresso grounds, French press grounds,
single pour-over grounds), and at your own risk
barbered me, and spread rank chickenshit
to feed me, I gave you Christ's wounds
and grew over you like Sleeping Beauty!"

They occur at a cellular level, occur
like insect generations in the grass:
infinitesimal changes . . . why should I feel
outside of it? Held above the stream?
At night when sentences finally blur

into cinema, the volte-face
of my life is a sacramental dream
of mudflat, estuary, spate, and spiel.

When I clutched that rock in the sea
off the Lido degli Artisti, and let
the surf rough me up, I didn't know
I was scratching my sunburnt skin
on rash-inducing medusa larvae.
That was no dream. More appropriate
than the beach chair I squirmed in
would have been a leper's lazaretto.

Yet that too passed—unsightly midriff,
infernal itching, paradisiacal holiday,
all together. I've planted, on the trellis's
other side, a Mlle. Geneviève Godard.
She'll be a rouge-tipped white, if
the description is correct, and meet halfway
the Don Juan's diabolical red. Scarred
gardeners make no promises.

STORM WINDOWS

The first was a fair youth
clutching a loaded Brown Bess.
In his pockets, iron hanks and hooks
furred green with watercress.

Then a lady in a farthingale . . .
Some strolled out of the surf,
some tumbled to the shore
at a king tide's royal rebuff.

Each time a squall passed through,
a window opened. In furbelows
and jewels they came;
in drenched velvet doublets and hose.

They had danced the tarantella,
the gigue, the allemande,
but found that a bell on the seafloor
can't make a sound.

I knew about the shipwrecks.
I shuffled up the lacy spiral
of the lighthouse steps.
Its shadow, like a sundial,

fell on the migrant dunes,
telling us where we stood—
the hour of the Anthropocene.
I put up my hood

against the wind. The light
warmed the iron rails;
traced the smile of the horizon
filled with toothy sails.

Beneath the breakers
was a strongbox, a tankard,
a hogshead of oil, a butt of beer—
cider, wine, ordnance, lard

for the lamps. At least one
encrusted Queen Anne pistol.
Belt buckles. Buttons. Coins.
They grew a sea gristle.

But I saw no ghosts, felt no tug
at my hem, and the whispers
of those strange words
like *sextant*, like *vespers*,

were dredged from my throat,
from terms whereunder

I could fathom my share
in the life they surrender.

Now twirling the rod, widdershins,
to make the slats lift on the blind
ruling the landscape, I write, I must,
where but in its settled dust?

BAD FORM

What did the arborist say?
That the tree had "bad form"
—which cut me to the quick.
The foliage-heavy sway
posed a danger in a storm.
It was tall where it should be thick.

Worse, it had bifurcated.
A limb had made a play
for equality with the trunk.
Now two trunks weighted
the odds against the day
that one would be sunk

in a hurricane-force wind
or just a microburst.
Since each was shaded
on one side, who'd sinned
against symmetry first
could be fruitlessly debated.

Meanwhile, squatting under
the self-divided sweet gum

was my house, my kids' bedroom.
Should it someday thunder
down as it grew—ad libitum—
it could spell their doom.

Weary, weary of responsibility
for the tree, which I thought
should take care of its
own form, I cursed witlessly
its shade. Which I never sought.
Where its phantom limb sits,

even now (the warning it sent
to tell me something's amiss).
Like a self-leafing book
in an act of sortes, its absent-
minded rifling of oasis
takes the form the breeze took.

IN THE NURSERY

*My mother always said we wear
our dreams—all living things . . .*
—Robin Robertson

Just now I go out and almost faint:
the moon waxing full (you can see
through windows in the clouds).
Where the statue of a saint
in old neighborhoods would be
are mulch, and rocks, and clods

of manufactured dirt without
a human face, or facsimile thereof,
to familiarize the plot. Yet perfume
hangs in the air: a whiff of doubt.
It is the Don Juan, the rose of love
(or something like it) making a room

or boudoir of its arbor. It
has thrived there, a real rough,
rootstock now so thick only a
power tool could possibly get
between its thorns (profuse enough
to rival a saw's teeth, and vice versa).

Merry red roses, canted upwards
like goblets, rise from canes that curve
from the spine in riblike fashion.
Mademoiselle Geneviève Godard's
health is not so good—*ma pauvre!*
This heirloom wasn't bred for passion,

yet, as a climber, should have met
her counterpart halfway. And now
a bag of blood meal hasn't cured
her wilted look. The other—bred
in the Hitchcock fifties—somehow
stays beefy, suave, and manicured.

When I went back to the nursery,
pleased that what they'd sold me
took so well, *took so well*
to the hot climate and poor soil
with which we were blessed,
which I had understood to be a test

of *my* skill . . . the garden adviser
shook his head. It would be wiser,
he said, not to grow anything close by,
and gave a stare. As to why
I can't sell you another one, there's
a wait list now. New plants are scarce.

I said it must be old to be so hardy
even in this zone. He demurred:
its vigor came from being *modern.*
"I'll tell you, we have a lot to learn
from those guys who scour cemeteries,
abandoned farms, old apothecaries'

botanicas . . . gentlemen, amateurs
spurred by a mania for cultivars

from centuries past. Lady, it's best
if you prune yours, keep it regressed.
It hears confessions, and grows
to bedroom heights." (Oh, *rose.*)

"And further, if the roots don't dig
under the house and re-twig
indoors via cracks in the foundation,
there's still damage being done,
and history will bear witness
with numberless lifted eyelids."

"As you probably know, Empress Josephine,
unable to give Napoleon an heir, retired
to Malmaison to grow roses, which shades
science into art, but back then even more—
excuse me—cutting-edge. When she died,
her estate, rosarium included, went to ruin.

Yet in its heyday of Cuisse de Nymphe Emue,
it was tended by Scottish botanists; specimens
from the Royal Botanic Gardens at Kew
were allowed past the naval blockades.
Years later, a rose in the imperial gardens
at St. Petersburg was called Souvenir de la Malmaison.

Was it a cutting saved from that briared-
over palace? Meanwhile, like alchemists,
small-time breeders were trying for gold.
That is, true yellow. These mostly poor
men of cloth and family businessmen
poured all their hopes into this enterprise . . .

So much of rose lore depends on their mold,
quiet artisans, far from royal laboratories,
pollinating stamens with a paintbrush . . .
One such man—his father told him food
was better; the gardens of the rich had
only so much room for roses; indeed,

he died in poverty. But in a final push
to leave his daughter with a legacy—
he'd named Mademoiselle Thérèse Levet
after her—he got Jacotot's Gloire de Dijon
—itself said to be sired by Souvenir de la Malmaison—
and propagated a splendid, languishing breed.

At what point does crossing roses lay
a curse? First exiled from Malmaison,
then unsalable, unwanted. Perhaps,
in secret, these alchemists wished
something toxic into roses' genomic maps.
Certain daturas, almost extinguished

because they killed their own pollinators,
have survived by means of the botanist
who didn't understand their powers.
Their elfin, shape-shifting flowers,
not easily identified, have been known
to poison pets and give visions to children

who unwittingly consume the honey
made by wasps which visited their stores.
It's possible that in pursuit
of perfumes that could intoxicate,
roses were embedded with scopolamine,
and planted like assassins."

What is this fardel of incidents
featuring entrepreneurial botanists,
imperial behests, a barren queen,
et in Arcadia ego? We make sense
by reverse engineering what exists
into fairy tales? "Have you seen

bees buzzing around Don Juan?
. . . Ah. Thought not.
Mademoiselle's Crépuscule des Âmes
is a kind of erethism; she's made wan
from his vitality. Sounds like a plot
(forgive me) out of Henry James

in your own backyard!" *Chortles.*

I haven't been back to the nursery since.

There's this to add:

Late in the year, the police chief detains
the much-older husband/
father of a woman and girl whose bodies

are found stabbed, bludgeoned,
and staged in their home. Song dies
on the lips. The radio rains and rains.

That summer, Mlle. Goddard
throws up a leafless, thornless stalk
like a snakebird. It grows nine feet
and because the thing could retard
the whole shrub, clip by clip I take
it down, adding its one effete

white blossom to the compost.

NAPLES, FLORIDA

A storm breathes—down our necks,
yes, but also oxygenated
by its warm air intake. As it knocks

about the Bahamas, ours is bated;
fresh water "flies off the shelves,"
and the coast by decree evacuated,

for we will not recuse ourselves,
not even at the peninsular end,
where the landmass calves.

Meanwhile, who can gainsay this friend,
the rosy armadillo, that surfaces?
And this katydid big as my hand,

greener than cotyledons; surpluses
of dragonflies with hematite
ball-bearing eyes, and tortoises

that one must run out to in the night,
in the lightning, to save when they've
dropped, as from an Aeschylean height,

midcrossing? As likely to wave
a flag of surrender as to appreciate
my dash into the road, the autoclave-

like contraption hissed in its breastplate.
I delivered it to the long grass
just as the ground issued an intimate

low Florida mist like laughing gas
that hides the passage from this world
of cold-eyed underlings in balaclavas.

MINIATURE HORSES
IN FLORIDA

....

I'm told the grass wicks up the lime
        underneath the pastures,
and that grazing it strengthens bone.
A blanket gift from geologic time.
        That's why in past years
horse breeding here has grown,

as has demand for attorneys of equine
        law, governing the long syringe
of parentage and fiduciary parties,
no less whimsical and byzantine
        because all consequences hinge
on the silent nonsignatories.

(Did the miniatures horses, say,
        have any input when they were bred
to grace the close perspectives
and take our breath away
        on roads they'd be electrified to tread?
But they too loved their ornamental lives.)

Springs glossed over the osteoid landscape.
        The long line at the women's toilet

didn't preclude girls picking their ear,
scratching a bite, adjusting a strap
      —such care lavished on the feet—
twitching at the utilitarian mirror.

Amid the trees and horripilated flora,
      in reverse-duckling fashion,
I trailed behind two boys—one my son—
their lengthening strides and hair a
      manifesto of dispassion,
a teenage state of abandon.

PART III

VENICITIS

The comic journals laughed at the pale, languishing victims of "Adriaticism," "Florencitis," and "Venicitis."

—Francis Steegmuller, *Flaubert and Madame Bovary*

THE ELEGANCE OF PELICANS

Along the fishing pier that dashes into the Gulf at Naples
on legs like a stop-motion photograph of a runner
multiplied at speed, lace-making waves swishing at his ankles,
three pelicans lunged at a blowfish that managed to
unhook itself from a lure, and adding feat to feat,
bewildered the ravenous birds by puffing itself up

so that the pelican that caught it startled; another took it up,
only to drop it instantly, and with half of Naples
looking on, cheering, the third gave it a try, and met defeat.
As they disported, thwarted, the blowfish like a rubber
ball allowed itself to be passed and dribbled from one to
another until, finagling its own interception at the ankles

of its opponents, it shrank, and sank among the barnacles.
This story, from the correspondence of Elizabeth Bishop,
is rather like the incident related in *Mozart's Journey to
Prague,* about two boating parties in the Bay of Naples.
Only one of them was stocked with girls. A rudder
pointed right at them, and a basket at their feet

stocked with oranges suggested a defense. Playfully, fête
galante style, the girls pelted the boys' ankles
with flying oranges, and athwart a slender rider

of the waves pitching, yawing, and rearing up,
each pulled off a volley for the passeggiata of Naples,
with great finesse and mirth, hand-to-

hand across the gunwales. There was a band, too,
playing saltarelli and canzoni against the buffet
of oranges, the flashing azure of the Bay of Naples,
which lifted the lace hems at the girls' ankles
as it rocked them. When the boys climbed up
into their boat, one took the prettiest, and rid her

of her cad. (A sail unfurled, depicting Cupid.) A reader,
accounting for the change in sensibility across two
centuries, might still conclude they don't add up.
But between the feat of the blowfish and the feat
of the suitors on the wavelets, a chime as of anklets
is my cue to keep skimming pages for more of Naples.

Like an underground runner of wild fruit, Naples
creeps up to your feet, bursting through the soil
to clap you by the ankles and start flowering!

DON GIOVANNI

It is eighty degrees in December.
It is he, on one of his furloughs,
bringing himself—and hell—up to date.
        My Don Juan, the better climber
(as the mercury yo-yos)
        is in a newly roused state,
the world circumcised away
from an out-of-season bud
leaving at the scrupulous rim—
        as it unfurls—a darker appliqué,
like O positive frozen solid
        at the sight of one's resuscitated victim.

This rosebush assiduously forks over
its works where most grandifloras falter,
thriving as far into the year as Capricorn.
        While named after a lover,
it decorates its own altar
        and wields an extraordinary thorn:
once I saw it catch a football
in those semiquaver quasi teeth;
it is three-headed, like Cerberus,

a hybrid drawing bloodlines from a root ball
on hands that all that's impure lies beneath.
      Hands can train it, barbarous

as it is, on an arbor, and I might like
to take its thick canes in harness,
first pouring cement as a base
      (so it knew I meant business).
Always poised to strike,
      they eventually undo their stays,
baying out like a window
of garnet, as at Chartres
(torture chamber in its basement,
      or so I hear). I wonder how
such a daemon rose got its start,
      what fairy tale explains its scent . . .

And then I go out tonight
and find him, swiping right
on every pretty face in candlelight.
      It's almost Christmas. Stacks
of square plates. (It's open-plan.) Tall racks
      of bottles. The whites and blacks,
clear glass, and stainless steel sieves
denote compliance with standards.
A wire basket of freckled pears

is transparency; sterilized knives
give full disclosure; and as regards
      the stemware, due diligence dares

a slip, especially on chanteuses like these
salting down from state-of-the-art speakers.
(Or is it sugar?) Does the chorizo flambé
      not deter him? Gold as all hell, valkyries
stand tall with beer to the brim. Beakers
      in siren form flush with Chianti, if not ambi-
valence. Recalling the steel meshes
belting Monterosso's
cliffs against the Vox
      Dei of the sea, the myth refleshes:
ordering, in the manner of heroes,
      an Andromeda on the rocks.

It's an adulterer's town, you see,
with warrens—if not warrants—
everywhere . . . stairs to a conspiracy
of fountains foiling the hearing
(while raking in the hush money)
. . . cul-de-sacs, a low clearing
where the costliest bottle decants
inside steak houses, doorways'
velvet drapes imparting *olés*;
the lacquered black of sport-
utility vehicles awaiting an escort,
if not a suited-up and damned
soon-to-be-subpoenaed maenad . . .

And all this complements
implacable monuments
at the ends of sight lines
to single-point perspectives—
massive pillars and paradigms
of statues and glyphs
dating back to temples and herms—
plus the bollards and berms
in the event of a truck bomb scare.

Fair enough that bringing her there,
then, you would feel served,
and falter, and be unnerved . . .

The sky of light concrete,
the rained-on concrete below,
the scuttling, indiscreet,
when accosting the hotel window
in a vague sort of recon
you beheld the street corner
where a lonely number met
a single letter of the alphabet.

ACCORDING TO OVID, THE HOTTEST SUMMER ON RECORD

....

*(*Metamorphoses, *Book II)*

I

If a Legend from
fell through a Prizm
joyriding Mustangs
Aethon, and Phlegon
half of California?
spent in engines
could raise ocean temps
then should we say

the sun's Blazer
came into Focus
Pyrois, Eous
might it ignite
If all the fossil fuel
in the span of a century
by a degree
we've been here before?

Clouds began to smoke
and made therewith so dry
from pastures
Corn combusted
Folk burned
New deserts arose

Earth flared
the green just disappeared
Leaves, trees were burned clean
Mighty towns roasted
Hardwoods turned to ash
and islands joined.

II

Athos, Taurus Timolus, Ida
Helicon the Muses' haunt
Haemus Orpheus's neighborhood
Parnassus, Eryx Cynthus, Othrys
Rhodope and its ski trails Mimas, Dindyma
Mycale, Cithaeron Scythia's cold nights
the snowcapped Caucasus Apennines, Alps.

All their big game and small fled
into the cracks of the earth to Hades
where the glaciers trickled down Vatnajökull
Jostedalsbreen, Chenega Chimborazo.

The nymphs' hair went up Springs boiled away
Boeotia looked for its Dirce Argos for its Amymone
Ephyre for its Pyrene The rivers steamed
Meander, Eurotas Euphrates, Ganges
The gold in the Tagus melted Nile, Rhine, Rhône
the Danube, the Po the sovereign Tiber.

The Cyclades became one as the sea shrank
stranding dolphins, seals Bream went belly-up

and cooked on the sands   Medusas desiccated
Reconnoitering birds   asphyxiated.

Earth's every volcano   became more so
the Moon stunned   that the Sun had come between them.

III

Once the Hummer, Explorer   Escalade, whatnot
was smote necessarily   as explained to the parents
the car crashed   the axle smashed
there were still those   who lamented the kid
The bitter father   The mother
on whose wild grief   we cannot linger
The metamorphosis   of humanity was complete.

His sisters—Phaëthousa   Lampetië et al.—
wailed so   they turned into leafy poplars
weeping amber   to this day
For all the restitution paid   in amber and in shade
they were still condemned   by perfect strangers
for mourning   their stupid boy.

It was his cousin Cygnus   shied into an "uncouth fowl"
who shunned company   stayed out of the sky
haunting retention ponds   blackwater swamps
intracoastal waterways   cooling his eyes.

ARETHUSA, SWALLOWTAIL, CONTRONYM

Swamp cypress candled itself above the water
where Nereus's daughter
ID'd carnivorous-looking white blooms
and erect scarlet racemes
exciting an admiral, plus some
small yellow species, all sulfur and helium.

She even thought she saw a hummingbird
feasting on the bells of bright red—
less a creature
than a miniature
tourbillon tweezing a gap in the humdrum
space-time continuum.

Damselflies, appointed in turquoise,
daubed wrists and knees:
their easy familiarity
as intrusive as their beauty.
Beneath the surface, eelgrass
had a psychedelic pulse.

Arethusa took the plunge and with a shock
found herself under a shelf of rock.
The bubbling places—feeder springs—
drew her into their eddyings
and any toehold she could get
onto a slimed cypress root

proved too slick. A would-be lover,
Alpheus, went in after her.
Arethusa chased not chaste
was taken by her water waist
forever. Now a spicebush swallowtail
given bias to its flight with metallic blue detail,

sails between us where we sit
("Yours or mine?" you said:
"ta anima") staring for a while
at the star-shaped inlaid tile
where fountain jets cleave and rebuff
and like both lights and fireworks, go off.

It was a bouffant bee, almost as big as the rose it lit on—
and that's the point: so late in the season was it, that
"remontant"—reblooming through the summer—
any blossom now was a shrunken simulacrum. So I lit on
the issue of all this sunshine leading to overproduction:
the roses I had counted in their furibund overproduction
showing diminishing returns. Something was out of joint
about the whole project, the projection of éclat
out of proportion to the product, which the bee imbibes,
the bouffant bee, with its understated point,
and those waxen wings that soften like a Roman tablet—
those waxen wings dissolving in light—whereas in Sumer
it was wet clay with its right-to-left writing,
and Greece, stone with its left-to-right writing
(like characters driving to or back from the sea), *on lit*,
depending on the home ground of far-flung scribes
deriving a style or stylus or maillot or mallet—
but now it is late for a bee to be supping at the last ember
of an evening somersaulting from sepia to auburn
and the rose to be remontant as rain makes a sweep
(water tutoring me, or *tutoyant*, as they say in Dieppe:
on intimate terms), so late in the day that lodgers
leaving their rentals shrink to traces in beer makers' ledgers.

DEATH IN VENICE

In Miami, *Ave Maria*s are pending.
A prayer, a charm, a petition,
a mother-to-daughter transmission:
"Blessed be the fruit of thy womb."
Female mosquitoes are sending
a virus through uterus and skull,
reviving the old rhyme with *tomb*.
Rendering baby's brainpan null.

My first thought is selfish:
Thank god I'm past all that . . .
The worries, the growing fat
on no Châteauneuf-du-Pape,
on no raw Brie or shellfish.
The lost pyramids of *fruits de mer* . . .
With pleasure we served ourselves up
to be denied. Or given a scare.

Rain scratches across my vision
utter loss of indemnity,
open cisterns breeding calamity.
Then I think of something worse:

the sun bleaching all petition,
all condolence: the *papier bible* rustle
of leaves without verse,
of bark without epistle.

Can I glance away from the megalopolis—
its neuronal shape tapering into
the hard-luck rural? Look at this:
a dwarf sun sits on our wing,
which catches it at a jaunty angle,
like an elbow catching an eagle—
        a shrunken sun-king.

Yes, I think of dormant viruses waking . . .
up in the air, day after the election,
knowing you, my friend, are also taking
off into the blue blue. Over D.C.,
can you believe (of course you can)
a little turbulence just began . . .
        as if to shake us *free*.

Chesapeake inlets look like fingers
—steamed crabs' "dead man's fingers,"
as they called the inedible lungs
back in the day. Lighting in these aisles was
loucher, the yellow of nicotine;
here ice-blue LEDs are clean
        but hard on the retinas.

Passing over Appalachia, it's unclear
those ancient puckers of ground below
are elevations. Attached to the window
a hair—not mine. It's not a leap
to think of some traveler's head askew,
exchanging the privilege of a view
        for that of sleep.

But the Rumpelstiltskin that stirs,
slithers into the lowlands of the Carolinas;
the lakes that gather in the savannas
are the color of turtle soup. Lures
include false myrtle, the Frozen Charlotte . . .
Soon I'll touch down where you cast
        an absentee ballot.

Impeachment hearings displace
the usual programming. Emissaries
with instruments now to a provincial
Joseph Cornell box-writ-large concert hall
come, beguiling us with Slavic symphonies,
the mood both hothouse and ice palace.

Like the diva who danced for the brigand
on a fur laid in snow, I'm dressed up in
sequined blue velvet—from Beirut,
whose ateliers come and go with *le goût
du risque.* I give the *Pathétique* a spin
and await my entrée to its wonderland.

In mermaid dress Ms. Olga Kern
swans to the piano. The strong bare arms
and shoulders that give expression to
Tchaikovsky move with rubato,
as if the root word, *robbed,* warms
to playing as to speaking out of turn.

I get fuzzy. On larger stages, nations
tip their hand, but with what éclat
musicians showcase their treasure!
which resonates with truth to measure,
something no jargon can obfuscate—
craft and cause are one; it stations

itself above pettier resources.
It is the only *agape* anymore;
I dress up for it, as for church,
naturalized to onion dome and birch
iconostasis for the length of the score,
beyond the reach of "historical forces."

Now an encore of Rachmaninoff.
The conductor, half priest, half
lab technician, judging by his jacket,
has in turn adjudged this racket
to be fair—he bows even to us riffraff
who applauded wrong, our timing off.

DANSE MACABRE

I hear a rattletrap, tread-worn, gear-shifting skeleton
(on the figure-eight trail where the mangroves jaw)
cycle by each time with a bigger, merrier peloton.

Such appearances infect us with a curious élan.
He's an ectomorph who fills the villages with awe.
I hear a rattletrap, tread-worn, gear-shifting skeleton.

The bicycles themselves look like clavicles driven
by breakneck couriers wearing a team bandanna,
cycling by each time with a bigger, merrier peloton.

The rust-speckled frame, the clacking chain
belie the leader's dash, his sangfroid.
I hear a rattletrap, tread-worn, gear-shifting skeleton

—but the wire basket, what use could it have when
it acts like a sieve for the ashes? It's a fundamental flaw
that goes unnoticed by the merry peloton.

And stuck in the busy spokes with a clothespin—
are those spades, and did you, kiddo, draw
that hand from the deck of the skeleton
that shuffles around nightly with his merry peloton?

CORDON SANITAIRE

Hester Prynne was a great Venetian,
stitching those rococo masks of hers in
—what was it, Salem? Concord?—
arduously embroidering toward
her eventual return to the fold . . .
Every stitch a step, every step foretold
by a design still hidden in things
—or should we say masqueradings,

as cardinals join the sewing circle,
then bluebirds with their Creamsicle
bibs. Even the plain homespun wren
and sparrow have masks; they warn
me to put on my own. I try on theirs,
they try on mine; each embroiders
the air with its signature, shoots the breeze,
as Hester sews another with intricacies

like the rubrics of illuminated manuscripts,
bindweed coiling through hearsay and tips,
dirt and buzz. The bluebirds on the fence

look for words, I mean worms, to mince.
One mask is a gingham and floral rigmarole,
another denim, another a kind of origami
of Venetian paper, such as Hester Prynne
would have studied for its pattern.

I catch a glimpse of the bird-within-a-bird
that, seen from below, is white embroidered
on its shadow self, its own dark side
or like its groom self basted to its bride.
The cardinal's note pierces the fanfare;
he pauses in the leafage before making a pair
with an unassuming female. Hester
doesn't make like a camouflaging nester:

She's flamboyant, x'ing out the rules
("on a field, sable, the letter A, gules")
—"embroidering," as if thereby
remaking rule as sumptuous lie.
I sit, a silhouette, behind the porch screen,
trapped, while the trapezoids of green
deepening with shade cannot withhold
sparrows from returning to the fold.

Now human speech is overdubbed
by winged droplets of sky subdued
into bluebirds. Now instead of blithe,

they're anxious, almost out of breath.
Night is falling. Forced by the pinprick
abysses in our threadbare communal fabric
to wait for immunity at needlepoint,
we sit behind screens, or pay the penalty.

Hester Prynne embroiders her mask
while singers with their jeweled-flask
bodies make pass after pass across the borders
peeping back at us back-porch birders.
This cordon sanitaire between us
is determined less by microbes than by discourse.
Masked, every cardinal's a wild card as
a bluebird falls for its own reflection in the glass.

PART IV

THE PSYCHIC CAPITAL OF THE WORLD

Beautiful, yes, but not much company.

—Elizabeth Bishop

EGRETS, HERONS, CRANES, IBISES . . .

We don't have much time; what there is of it
seems slower because we're engulfed by sun
on a wide flat prairie whose grassy palette
conceals so much in its variegation

that our gaze takes a while to travel
across the vast swathe at our feet.
Were we to examine it on a swivel,
a circle would take an hour to complete—

the way the three-mile loop does. Birders
with cameras come from all over
to see the species transcend borders
for an exotic grub to discover,

or pond to plunder, fitted at birth
(as we are not) with a tiny magnet
to help align them with the earth,
the latitude-longitude dragnet

drawn out on our grade school maps—
or else they know to navigate by stars

on their cross-continental trips,
as attentive to pattern as to particulars.

At any rate, we come for the waterfowl,
mostly, who come for this water park,
hanging out to dry without a towel
or taking to the sky to make no mark.

Zero swans, French hens, turtledoves,
or partridges here, and mockingbirds
—spurning the afflatus of true loves!—
prefer places with more, not fewer, words.

When all falls away to sigh and murmur,
a lone anhinga commands a post:
in tux colors, he's conductor,
and gestures to the heavenly host,

shoulders risen, wings extended.
Really, there's something not funny at all
—just too human—in the unbefriended
sounds that issue from the caterwaul:

a bleat, a bleep, a honk; a syrinx fissile,
deviated, its signal lapsed into wind . . .
yet each bird (to our eye so replete a vessel!)
strains to hear another of its kind.

Cuban brothel music played
while we ate affogato:
cold espresso over ice cream.
Double-paned windows betrayed
a world whipped to and fro
as by a double-crossed dream.

In the flotsam of my handbag
was a double reed for bassoon:
difficult, costly, a talisman
swimming in the depths I'd drag
for loose change, tissues, picayune
lists, receipts, hairpins, and fan . . .

I rehearsed the phrase I like:
these storms are said to "organize"—
the way the fitful mind awaits
the moment thought will strike
and tries on sentences for size
till something takes, or sates.

Incredibly, an intelligence
comes to animate the words.

When the storm begins rotations
counterclockwise, do we sense
a formal order it is working towards
even as it wrecks our towns?

What I need is a double read
of the hurricane. What fagotto—
as houses shred to toothpick,
and no god takes heed,
and we glut ourselves on affogato—
plays such breakup music?

POSSIBLE SEA BREEZE
COLLISION IN THE
EVENING HOURS

A tango record's record
of scratches and scuffs
matches the dance floor's,
where women—walked backward
to 1920s Buenos Aires—
put their foot down. *His* sole buffs

the wood *her* little heel makes
half-moons in, so hard and soft
go back and forth in the atelier;
he pushes, and she brakes.
As the music carries them aloft,
all of life seems statelier.

Now, Carlos Gardel knew a myth
is the simplest amplifier;
stoking his fangirls' flame,
he hid the woman he was with
out of the line of fire
in a secret hacienda; laid claim

to Uruguay as native land and muse;
avowed that his mother was a widow.
But she was an unmarried *fille*.
A record of his birth exists in Toulouse.
All of which must go to show
the better stories tend to be iffy,

the three-minute arias ring true—
if three minutes is about as long
as we can hold our breath;
and for all the dancing à deux
we hand each other off for a song,
digging in our heels at death.

Cheek by jowl, these subdivisions
live amid the remnants
of the farms they have replaced.
Tongue in cheek, the signage runs
"Rip van Winkle Ranch,"
with no real sense of haste.

A grazing bull would stand
in its paddock, undisturbed
beside the road—until
"Bull for sale: one grand,"
meaning he'd been served,
and eventually went spectral.

The day of the full eclipse
milling crescents in the shadows,
we sat on a bench and saw
only each other; then the tips
of a bull's horns, in twos,
charged everything with awe.

Heaven's china shop might be
stampeded by those wraiths

as the celestial plates aligned.
It was the last thing some would see;
blame solar retinopathy
for the thing that made us blind.

A ship of cows, en route
from Uruguay to Syria, sank
that December near Beirut—
each wave trying to outrank
the last before slamming the seawall
with the surge of a cattle call.

At the picture window, I watched.
What did I expect: that cows
would rebound out of the surf,
rescuing themselves, patched
from tankers and scows
and give themselves up for beef?

A few miles south, Jove hid
in a bull (what is myth trying to tell us?).
Our labyrinthine lives, hybrid
of economy and transport,
are enough to make me jealous
of when we were the gods' sport . . .

I could see the neon hotel sector
where convoys were brought to bear

on headland curves; the deck chairs
cleared for milongas; nectar
of night blooms in the hair
advancing international affairs.

IT DECIDES TO RAIN

....

. . . che sanza speme vivemo in disio.
            —Dante

Waiting for the sky to lighten,
    I watched a star slide like a tear
from one pane to the next—
    a day after the harvest moon,
deceived as to the hour
    on a night already vexed

with too much clarification.
    Once it was light enough
to see his face, I would have
    to leave. My desolation,
in spite of our love,
    he thought not very brave;

chafing against the limits
    of our lives, none too wise.
We were poised to do no little harm.
    But where I lay I thought it's
what takes us by surprise
    that persuades us of its charm,

and not the light it sheds.

When I get up to go, no one's
the wiser; and unanswered

longings hang by threads
to words, in questions

we put long ago to bed.

"THE ONLY PARADISE
IS A LOST PARADISE"

A brooch is out of fashion. Perhaps as much so
as Cupid kneeling to Psyche, in this art nouveau
vintage replica, goldtone with rollover
clasp that holds its bodkin like a sleeping lover
or a latch across a door, laid in its crook
ever so gingerly. Well, she has doffed her cloak,
with one arm raised in a flourish. His wings
wait—crossed behind his back, like fingers,
though he isn't false, exactly.
            Not even the store
where it cost a fin is open anymore.

He took her to these out-of-the-way places
so as not to be seen. There were Muses in relief
on blue Wedgwood. Uranium glassware in cases
under black light. Jewelry that would spook a thief.
Florida Highwaymen paintings, sold in gas stations,
he told her, in the fifties, with pimped-out palms
against Curaçao seas, sunset conflagrations
brighter than hurricane lamps.
Louder than Fat Tuesday.
            It burned to the ground,

the antiques palace. For worse or for better,
it was only there that the lovers had found
a counterfeit for growing old together.

....

Like chimneys rising from an incandescence
kindled by brass elevators, these buildings
go up, and up, in concentric rings
from a storied point of reference
and—in this season—twinkling lights.
Dearest, simply circling the blocks
catching sight of gilt spruces in foyers ignites
Nutcracker fantasias, with elfin cuckoo clocks.

Shiny, shiny, the river's hammered ribbon.
It twists to show one nap, then the other,
along a path where promenaders tie one on,
wrapping Roosevelt Island in ether.
Then there's the comedy of pooches
at the dog park, also wrapped—in ponchos,
charging each other like reindeer
hurtling from balcony to belvedere.

Occasionally in beveled glass I glimpse a dram
of Venice, a teaspoonful of Amsterdam,
or the garbage scow that reinvents
itself as a wintry river's sled of presents.
That is to say, it's no big leap

from traipsing through a storybook
to feeling like a ghost. In my sleep
I'll see the honey-and-gaslight look

of a faux nineteenth-century sconce
through the window of a cab,
rain-strafed and foggy near where I once
lived. After the glass of wine I'll grab,
the sky will gray into a citywide utility.
Sore-throated, I'll spot a dispossessed tree
lying in the street, its scent yet unexhausted,
pointing the way its mugging angels fled . . .

I shore my dreams up when I waken.
Shouldn't life resolve, like the acronym
by which the twice-shy Levin
swayed Kitty to marry him?
Shouldn't life contain such loves—
the "alder leaf f, the unripe apple of p"
—as synesthetic Nabokov's,
whose rainbow spelled k-z-s-p-y-g-v . . . ?

THE SIRENS HAVE
STOPPED SINGING

....

Now the sirens have a weapon that is still more terrible
than their singing, which is to say their silence.
—Franz Kafka

I stepped in out of the cold, at loose ends,
on a day the temps had fallen—
fallen below a threshold I could stand
or even walk in (as ice intends
us more or less to glide when
hazarding snowflake-fairyland).

Who knew I was gliding toward
the heaven of disused instruments?
Flutes and clarinets in glass cases,
a whole floor of harpsichord
and piano, with open vents
to steel guts. (Those ivory grimaces,

that jumble of multiple legs:
it might have been a rustled herd
sending up a silent wail.) Displays

of hand-carved mutes, tuning pegs,
and chin rests conferred
dignity to accoutrements. (The days

of accoutrements are all but over.)
And then there was the odd thing
any craftsman would redact—
an openwork bell that couldn't cover
the bare requirements for a ring;
a woodwind like a digestive tract.

Prettiest of all were the viol, lute,
and harp, each fashioned with a head
(female, coiffured in wood and ivory)
leaning into negotiations so acute—
I drew close to hear what was being said,
from which there will be no recovery.

My mother, in 1966, is an accessory
atop a Revolutionary War cannon:
leopard print coat, buttons undone,
legs slimly pressed, bare knees closed—
a scene both faded and overexposed.
She wasn't used to winter; vis-à-vis
her status as "permanent resident alien,"
she should have covered up. Pennsylvania . . .
Her brother already drafted in the army.
The very picture of a White Russian!
But not *Pale Fire*, not *Uncle Vanya*,
not tsars and ballerinas, *les vieux pays*.
Why it should feel scandalous, dunno—
not yet twelve, she'd come from São Paulo.

Perhaps three continents in a dozen years
seems extravagant or suspicious:
shady characters under the oranges
committing to a death pact or an alias;
speaking, in code or third languages,
of wartime escapades that we, all ears,
wouldn't learn from books or on the street.
The stories were always incomplete,

like the gaps in a country ballad:
Did he find her in the Cold Kentucky Rain?
Did the Most Beautiful Girl in the World
ever come home? It drove me mad
in the backseat: the songs unfurled
to a compass rose's points of pain.

A water tower just beyond her yard
overlooks the wintry town as far
as thin, brown French Creek.
That's how I can find my way back
once I cross the bridge. It's hard
to get Wi-Fi, except in a wine bar,
where Dylan's "Mozambique"
jangles in the cavernousness. Malbec?
At loose ends, the bartender explains
(or pitches . . .) his product is local,
from vineyards here where I was born.
But, I think, between erratic rains
and freezes, this climate is equivocal,
too encouraging to the stubborn.

In my youth I fled into the vast park,
lush, even in winter, with pale grassy
wheat-like ripplings over its broad hill
rolling back a wind of *thee*s and *thou*s
to the spotlit banner in the dark:

a teen listening for an embassy.
Now the Valley Forge carillon starts to play
a lament for bells melted for artillery.
The streets are named after generals—
Rochambeau, LeBoutillier—
names we hardly knew how to say:
a boutonniere or fritillary
stab at littler chimes or spells
dissipating into funerary air . . .

Rendezvous had a Southern twang
in 1976; what emitted from the dash
salted me with something huge
and vaguely unseemly; what they sang,
for all that, came with an eyelash
unbatted at the subterfuge.
Think of Edna O'Brien's
"The reason love is so painful is that
it always amounts to two people
wanting more than two people
can give." It isn't rocket science . . .
escape velocity is exactly what
revolutions pledged: liberty to roam.
Songs asked, *When are you coming home?*

APPROACHING THE GROUND

With a dolly and a zoom, the Airbus
entire Everglades shows us:
blotchy cloud-shadows thrown
on seepage algae's overgrown.

Observe—the air we freely breathe
from this height seems to sheathe
the earth in miasma. The clouds look
like dross. The Everglades look

like dross. Biomass is, essentially, dross.
In Miami, all the gold that could enclose
a woman's finger, wrist, or neck
was on display, as if to deflect

knowledge of her own mossiness.
Pretend not to know what this says
about our aspirations to the high life.
Up in the Airbus, I see as if

for the first time how a cloverleaf
turns a highway into a motif
on the margins of a manuscript
illuminated with a wing that tipped

itself in asphalt. The story it tells
wants unstapling into angels,
heavenly bodies drawn raptly in
on tailwinds, touched with halogen.

WATTEAU

"No Trespassing," read the blackened sign,
prompting a wry laugh. Scorched earth brooks no law.
The blazes happened months ago in the news.
Now a wilderness prodigal with chartreuse,
fresh brushwork as far as Santa Barbara,
brilliantly set off the carbonized pine.

Incendiaries go where they are sent.
It wasn't just expensive landscape daubed
with embers; after, winter torrents ground
raindrops through whirlwinds to thunder on the ground.
Mudslides came to heavy rest. Mushrooms knobbed
new doors for the permanent resident.

Fires even crept toward the Getty,
where you and I walked. Bridal travertine's
a flame-resistant dress for art veiled in glass.
The sprinkler system half-camouflaged in grass
wasn't for the drought-friendly evergreens,
but defense against glowing confetti.

Item 1: The Wonder Cabinet.
Doors and drawers ajar, it seemed to say
there was nowhere to hide; given a scare,

every eye in its head returned such a stare
that a dovecote emptied at once. (Judgment Day.
All Souls'. Debts discharged to the Infinite.)

Item 2: Venus. Someone wake her
(as Bacchus and the maenad are doing)
so she can flee the place where her nudity
draws out the peeping fruit of the lemon tree.
Perhaps its light cologne is so wooing
that she'll deliquesce before flames take her.

Item 3: *La Surprise.* A Watteau
recovered after two hundred years is
possibly retardant. Tuning his guitar,
the musician observes two lovers; they are
oblivious. Beyond, a precipice
drolly cleaves the picture plane in two.

(The dog, a bit player, sides with *him*.)
You're still too green to share my despair
that Wonder, Love, and Art each represent a stage.
The far sensuousness of mist will engage—
like the blue plumbago that brushed our hair—
then dissolve into sexless seraphim.

THE MESOCOSM

Two sounds in the house lately:
clanking barbells and electric guitar
behind garage and bedroom doors.
J.'s mesocosm failed; he flagrantly
excused himself on the basis of gender,
as the gathering of mud and spores,

weeds and worms for "nurturing"
is not the métier, apparently, of boys.
Dear A., I myself was quite taken
with the idea that we can bring
a world to life like animated toys,
a sealed jar sustaining frog and fen.

So much for that. It's the fall equinox:
the radio broadcast Vivaldi twice.
I know the change by the slant of light—
slant of light + concerto. The clocks
quietly gallop. Maybe it's the promise
of achieving equilibrium, under tight

conditions, of carbon and oxygen
in give-and-take. I'm in dire need of
—what to call it?—magic. I worry

that Zoom is ruled by djinn
that filter out the wavelength of love
and so I wear my evil eye jewelry,

as you advised, against being too
much in view: that tiny frog on display . . .
(like the specimen I saw once
on a man's gold ring in Italy. Who
could wear that showpiece of the atelier?
Only, perhaps, a witty prince.)

Personal adornment is out anyway.
Yet the citrus trees have kept up
appearances (no shortage of lemons).
I watch the progress day after day
of those novitiate spathes that erupt
from the peace lily . . . a summons

from the offices of mediation. (Laws
are stipulated by plants too. See *stipule*.)
Occasionally a rare aircraft
lights up the tropopause.
Where is the workshop of the soul?
"His bed," I averred. You laughed.

Those late spring nights the street
was overrun with frogs, I walked with care:
a purse, a pulse . . . a pulse-in-a-purse

mimicking the heart that skipped a beat
or made a choice in error
it couldn't, then or now, reverse.

Cold-blooded hearts everywhere I stepped!
Lentil-colored, stippled, with the froideur
of the ex-lover. What's one more plague?
Outside, it's too hot. Summer's overslept,
a season out of touch with the calendar.
The strip malls, dear A., exude nutmeg.

VENICE, FLORIDA

The clouds went on each afternoon—
bodybuilding to a rippling mass,
flat-topped, or with bedhead;
from a puffball, picayune,
they did something to the grass
fluorescing on the watershed.

It rained so hard all summer long,
every field was canalized
by overflow, or turned into lagoon.
The fountain jets burped a song
of bullfrogs poolside, bull's-eyed,
prelude to a honeymoon.

Electricity's appendages, like
butterfly filaments, alit on things,
charging the soil with nitrogen,
so you'd run, as though Nike
grabbed your ankles by their wings,
and you were an Olympian.

On one of these afternoons,
you met your tennis coach,
storms needling the atmosphere,

clouds like hydroponic blooms,
roots whitening on approach.
You should have shown more fear,

hitting balls that greenly blazed
in the hyacinthine climate;
like statuary, your torso flexed
on tiptoe, your arm upraised
to execute a serve, until the wet
match fizzled out. (There's a text

that warns boys of hubris!)
Then things would clear.
A dragonfly would gondolier
through the misted air and seem
to offer a golden balance beam
to the showboating iris.

A calmness floods the aftermath.
This is the secret of summer eves,
when ultramarine bands the earth,
twin to the blue hour in the north.
Not snowfields, but grass and leaves
dusk milks blue for all they're worth.

ACKNOWLEDGMENTS

....

Grateful acknowledgment to the editors of the following publications, where these poems first appeared: *Liberties*, *LitMag*, *London Review of Books*, *The New York Review of Books*, *The Paris Review*, *Plough*, *PN Review*, *Poetry*, *The Sewanee Review*, *The Southern Review*, *The Times Literary Supplement*.

Parts of "Death in Venice" first appeared in *Poems for Political Disaster*, published by the *Boston Review*.

"Sleepwalking in Venice" was reprinted in *The Best American Poetry 2019*, edited by Major Jackson and David Lehman.

Thanks to Erin O'Luanaigh and Rebecca Ariel Porte for reading this book in manuscript. To my literary colleagues at the University of Florida: *grazie mille*. A bow to Jill Ciment and Amy Hempel for taking me to Cassadaga ("the psychic capital of the world"). A research grant from the College of Liberal Arts at UF allowed me to travel. Jonathan Galassi gave me *coraggio*.